The Great Big Book of Life

Can you find ME every time you turn a page?

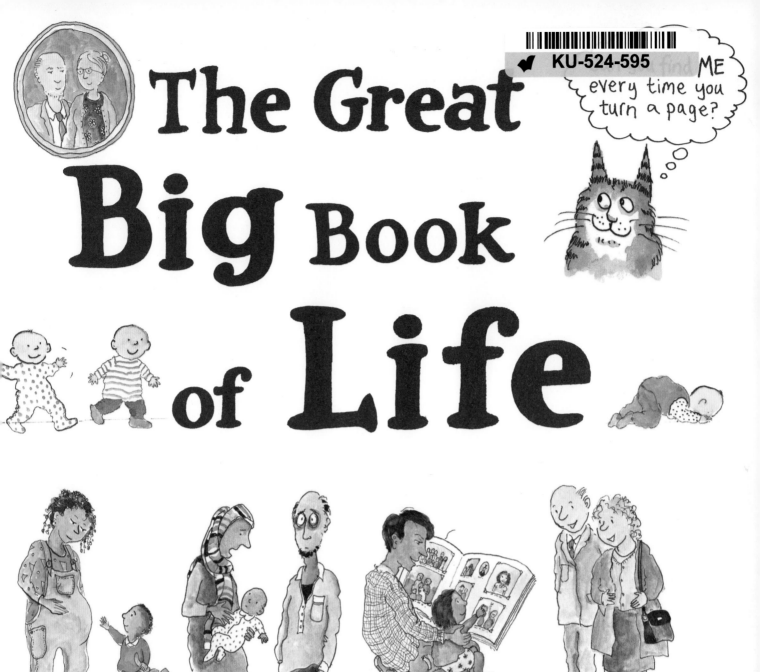

Mary Hoffman and Ros Asquith

Lincoln
Children's Books

HOW it all BEGAN

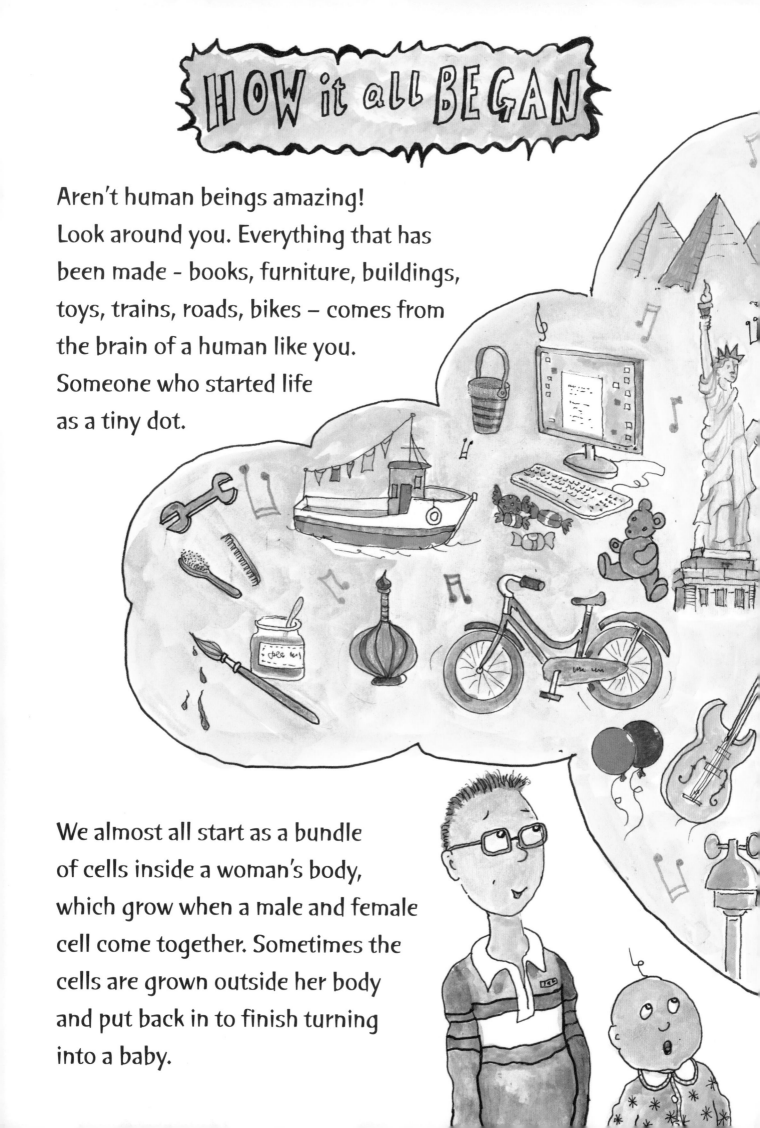

Aren't human beings amazing!
Look around you. Everything that has
been made - books, furniture, buildings,
toys, trains, roads, bikes – comes from
the brain of a human like you.
Someone who started life
as a tiny dot.

We almost all start as a bundle
of cells inside a woman's body,
which grow when a male and female
cell come together. Sometimes the
cells are grown outside her body
and put back in to finish turning
into a baby.

Being a BABY

It takes about nine months for a baby
to be ready to come out into the world.

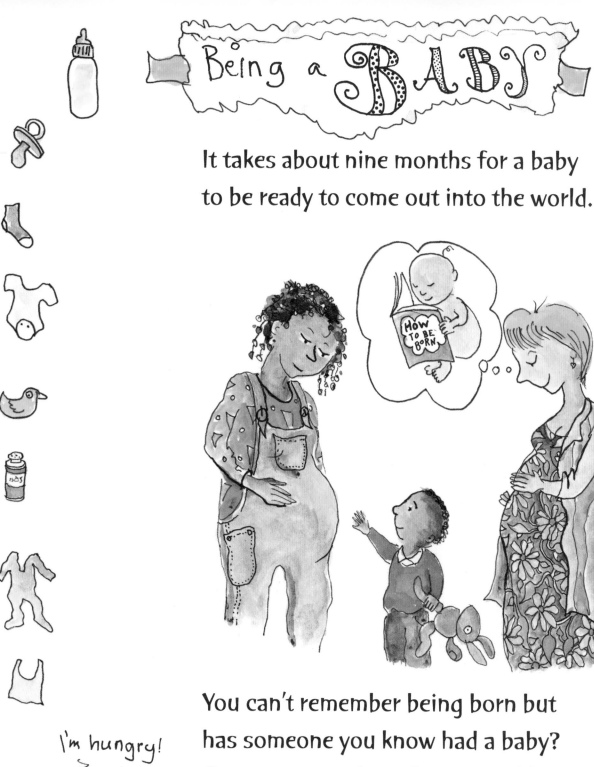

You can't remember being born but
has someone you know had a baby?
Can you remember what it was like
when they were born?

I'm hungry!

I'm too hot.

My bottom hurts.

I'm tired.

I'm wet!

Babies are so tiny and helpless they can't do anything for themselves except cry. It takes six weeks before they can even smile. And they certainly can't use words. So crying means everything.

I have to support his head, because he can't.

Six weeks old. Time to SMILE!

If human babies waited till they could talk and walk before they were born, they would be too big to fit in their mother's body or to come out easily.

I'm cold.

My tummy hurts.

I'm angry.

I'm scared.

I'm lonely.

Babies may be helpless, but they are very good at CRYING!

But in the weeks and months that pass
babies learn to recognise people and to smile,
to hold up their own heads, to turn themselves over,
to sit up and then to crawl.

They can clap their hands, blow bubbles,
chuckle with pleasure, frown, hold toys,
look at books, suck their thumbs, and twiddle
their hair. Soon they learn to pull themselves
up by holding on to bits of furniture.

And once they can walk, they are toddlers.

Whoops!

Shhh, you'll wake the baby.

If you know any babies, you will see they sleep a lot during the day. But the funny thing is – they don't sleep so well at night!

For at least the first six weeks, parents don't get much sleep either as someone has to get up and feed the baby a couple of times in the night. That's because babies' tummies are so small they can't drink enough milk to last them through till morning.

Granny says it's good for babies to sleep through noise.

LATER...

Shhh! You'll wake the baby!

Some babies take years to learn to sleep through the night – those are the ones with the really tired-looking parents.

Everyone needs a good night's sleep throughout their life to refresh their bodies and brains. If we don't get it, we can be miserable and cross all the next day.

Is she getting enough sleep?

She is. But I'm not.

Guess who had a good night's sleep?

EATING & DRINKING

For about six months, milk is all babies need to eat.

Then they start trying out new foods and get in an awful mess. It takes time to learn to handle a spoon and put the food in the right place.

We should never have dressed her as a princess. All she'll eat is strawberries and cream.

Some babies eat anything and others are really fussy. Just like grown-ups. We all have favourite foods and things we really don't like.

But we all need lots of different kinds of foods to keep us healthy and give us energy.

CATTO NOSH

HEALTHY FOOD

NUTS

FRUIT

VEGeTABLES

FISH

I think I'll stick with MILK for now.

New babies get colds very easily because their bodies haven't met diseases before and can't fight them off.

When babies are small, they are given injections called 'vaccinations.' They start getting their shots at a few months old. Measles, mumps, rubella and chickenpox used to be called 'childhood illnesses' but are less common now that babies are vaccinated.

Other illnesses, like TB, smallpox and polio are very rare now in countries where you can get vaccinations.

You don't need a doctor. You've just got a nasty COLD.

NASTY cold

NICE cold

Can flies catch GERMS? Do Mosquitoes get MALARIA? Do polar bears catch COLDS? Can SNAKES be POISONED?

If you do get sick, you can go to the doctor. But for some illnesses there is no injection and you can get things like colds throughout your life.

A-tishoO!

Use a TISSUE!

Between the ages of about two and three, little children start being able to control where and when they pee and poo.

No more NAPPIES. Hooray!

NAPPY BIN

Bye bye NAPPIES. Hurrah!

NAPPY BIN

Whoops...

NAPPY BIN

So their parents get them a potty or a smaller toilet seat. This doesn't always go smoothly and small people can have accidents or wet their beds for many years. But most people get there in the end.

Does 'oo want a poo poo on the potty?

No thank you. I'd prefer to use the toilet.

Some things our bodies do, like farts and sneezes, are much more difficult to control!

¡LOOK who's TALKING!

When babies start to talk, they babble all sorts of sounds. Then they learn which sounds have meaning in their language. They start with one word at a time and soon start combining them into longer phrases.

Waaa means I'm hungry.
Wooo means I'm wet.

Sadly, no one speaks CAT.

BABY TALK

Little children say funny things sometimes while they are learning to talk and invent brilliant words and names for their toys.

No! **MY** bibbly wibbly!

Boggle

Offilant

The younger you are, the easier it is to learn a second language. Some grown-ups find it hard. But in many homes families use more than one language.

Talking is only one part of language. We listen and read and write too.

There are just 26 letters in the English alphabet but we can mix them up to make thousands of words. It's strange to think that all poems and songs and books and plays and films are made up of so few letters.

What clever words you both make up.

No. I'm speaking Chinese and he's speaking Dutch!

We use sign language

Pwaney waney

Ooky

Is NOT Pwaney, is AIRPIN

Reading and writing become even more important when we start school. Most people go to school but some have lessons at home.

However you learn, it's important for the rest of your life. It helps you to get work, teaches you about the world and how to enjoy it. And it's where you make friends who may last for life.

School can seem as if it goes on forever – we start when we are four or five and leave when we are eighteen as quite different people.

But we are lucky if we have schools to go to. In many countries children don't.

ART

MATHS

No. I'll see you at 3 o'clock!

Bye Daddy. See you in 13 years time.

I wish I could go to school.

TEENAGE YEARS

Have you got a teenage brother or sister? The teenage years of life can be very stormy. From about the age of ten your body can start turning into a grown-up's before your mind and your feelings have caught up.

But you're a really NICE teenager.

TERRIBLE TEENS

Can I skip being a teenager and go straight to being an ADULT?

A teenage cat is an OLD cat.

Teenagers can be moody and changeable – or charming and helpful. Or both on the same day!

My Teenage Sister in a BAD mood.

My Teenage Sister in a GOOD mood.

They need a lot of sleep and get up late in the morning. And they often like to stay up late, listening to music and playing games.

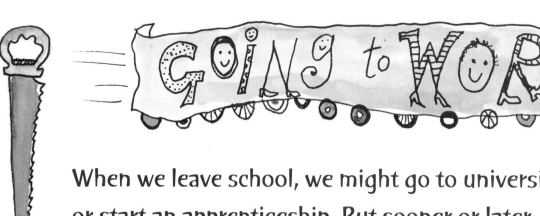

Going to WORK

When we leave school, we might go to university or start an apprenticeship. But sooner or later, usually by the time we've stopped being teenagers, we need to find a job.

Some people are lucky and find work doing something they love, at home or somewhere else. Others are not happy in their jobs.

And for many people it's hard to find any kind of work at all.

PARTNERS

Grown-ups often find someone they want to go out with and maybe even spend the rest of their life with. This might happen when they are teenagers or when they are much older.

My 32nd boyfriend. He could be the ONE.

Some people have lots of girlfriends or boyfriends before they settle on just one. And some never do!

The only person who asked me to get married was my MUM.

But you don't have to have a partner to lead a happy life.

When two people decide to spend their lives together they often want to have children. And so life starts all over again with babies!

But many people don't want to be parents and there are already so many people in the world that it's OK not to add any more.

Too many people. Too few CATS.

MIDDLE YEARS

When babies become teenagers, their parents
are in the middle years of life.

All sorts of things happen to them.
They may separate from each other
and find new partners and start
new families.

They may have great success at work
or they may get into trouble with the law
and have to spend time in prison away from
their families.

They may change careers or lose their jobs and have to find other work.

You're FIRED!

They may enjoy many things outside work, like dancing, or playing sport or making beautiful things.

Or they might just like going out with friends or to concerts or plays or festivals or on exciting holidays.

My kids have left home, so I can do whatever I want!

I never had kids, so I've been doing that for ages.

OLD AGE

Teenagers grow up and leave home and maybe start their own families. So the people who used to be parents themselves become grandparents!

It's so much fun being a grandparent. It means having all the good times with the new children but still getting a good night's sleep!

As people get older things may go wrong in their bodies or their minds. They may get ill or forget things.

Other older people stay fit and start new careers or hobbies. As long as they feel well, older people don't have to give up work – especially if they do a job that doesn't depend on being young.

DEATH

But in the end, all bodies wear out and people die. It's just as well because if everyone lived for ever there would be no space in the world for the new people being born.

Death is very mysterious and no-one really understands it. But it means that life has come to an end. The person stops breathing and their heart stops beating and the blood stops moving round their body. So they can't talk or feel or move any more. They have gone.

Have you ever had a pet who died? Cats and dogs have much shorter lives than we do so we'll all know something about death long before we reach our own.

He used to LOVE swimming about.

Sadly, some people die before they get old. They might have an accident or an illness and then they have a short life. Others live to be really old – over 100!

But we can remember people long after they have died – the kind of person they were and what they did and said in their life.

That's granny when she was your age.

BACK to the FUTURE

We may live on through our grandchildren, greatgrandchildren and ever so many descendants. Or we might be remembered for the things we did.

We all have a life worth living, whether we are rich or poor, famous or not, with a family or single.

Let's make the most of our lives and try to be happy and to make those around us happy too.

Life is for living – so enjoy every day!